50 Delicious Cooking Meals Recipes for Home

By: Kelly Johnson

Table of Contents

- Spaghetti Aglio e Olio
- Chicken Tikka Masala
- Beef Stroganoff
- Vegetarian Chili
- Shrimp Scampi
- Ratatouille
- Pork Tenderloin with Apples
- Creamy Mushroom Risotto
- Lemon Herb Grilled Chicken
- Tofu Stir-Fry
- Fish Tacos with Cabbage Slaw
- Quinoa Salad with Roasted Vegetables
- Baked Ziti
- Stuffed Bell Peppers
- Thai Green Curry
- Eggplant Parmesan
- Moroccan Chickpea Stew
- Honey Garlic Salmon
- Chicken Fajitas
- Vegetable Pad Thai
- Beef and Broccoli Stir-Fry
- Butternut Squash Soup
- Shrimp and Grits
- Caprese Salad
- Teriyaki Chicken Bowls
- Black Bean Tacos
- Spinach and Feta Stuffed Chicken
- Lasagna Bolognese
- Greek Salad with Grilled Chicken
- Coconut Curry Lentil Soup
- BBQ Pulled Pork Sandwiches
- Pesto Pasta Primavera
- Balsamic Glazed Brussels Sprouts
- Chicken Caesar Salad
- Vegetable Samosas

- Salmon Quinoa Bowl
- Chorizo and Potato Hash
- Indian Butter Chicken
- Zucchini Noodles with Marinara
- Falafel Wraps
- Sweet Potato and Black Bean Enchiladas
- Cilantro Lime Rice with Grilled Shrimp
- Beef Enchiladas
- Roasted Vegetable Quiche
- Mediterranean Grain Bowl
- Jambalaya
- Lobster Mac and Cheese
- Stuffed Portobello Mushrooms
- Chicken Noodle Soup
- Spicy Peanut Noodles

Spaghetti Aglio e Olio

Ingredients:

- 12 oz spaghetti
- 6 cloves garlic, thinly sliced
- 1/2 cup olive oil
- 1/4 tsp red pepper flakes (optional)
- Salt and pepper to taste
- Fresh parsley, chopped (for garnish)
- Grated Parmesan cheese (optional)

Instructions:

1. **Cook Pasta:** Boil salted water in a large pot. Cook spaghetti according to package instructions until al dente; reserve 1 cup pasta water and drain the rest.
2. **Sauté Garlic:** In a large skillet, heat olive oil over medium heat. Add garlic and red pepper flakes, cooking until the garlic is golden but not burnt.
3. **Combine:** Add the cooked spaghetti to the skillet, tossing to combine. If it seems dry, add reserved pasta water a little at a time.
4. **Season:** Season with salt and pepper. Serve with chopped parsley and Parmesan cheese if desired.

Chicken Tikka Masala

Ingredients:

- 1 lb chicken breast, cubed
- 1 cup plain yogurt
- 2 tbsp lemon juice
- 2 tbsp garam masala
- 1 tsp cumin
- 1 tsp paprika
- 1 tbsp oil
- 1 onion, chopped
- 4 cloves garlic, minced
- 1 inch ginger, grated
- 1 can (15 oz) tomato sauce
- 1 cup heavy cream
- Salt to taste
- Fresh cilantro (for garnish)

Instructions:

1. **Marinate Chicken:** In a bowl, combine chicken, yogurt, lemon juice, garam masala, cumin, and paprika. Marinate for at least 1 hour, preferably overnight.
2. **Cook Chicken:** Heat oil in a skillet over medium heat. Add onions, garlic, and ginger; sauté until softened.
3. **Add Chicken:** Add marinated chicken and cook until browned.
4. **Make Sauce:** Stir in tomato sauce and simmer for 10 minutes. Add heavy cream and season with salt. Simmer for another 10 minutes.
5. **Serve:** Garnish with fresh cilantro and serve with rice or naan.

Beef Stroganoff

Ingredients:

- 1 lb beef sirloin, thinly sliced
- 1 onion, sliced
- 2 cups mushrooms, sliced
- 2 tbsp flour
- 1 cup beef broth
- 1 cup sour cream
- 2 tbsp Worcestershire sauce
- Salt and pepper to taste
- Egg noodles for serving

Instructions:

1. **Cook Beef:** In a skillet, brown the beef over medium-high heat; remove and set aside.
2. **Sauté Veggies:** In the same skillet, add onions and mushrooms. Cook until softened.
3. **Make Sauce:** Sprinkle flour over veggies, stir, then gradually add beef broth. Bring to a simmer.
4. **Combine:** Return beef to the skillet, stir in sour cream and Worcestershire sauce. Season with salt and pepper.
5. **Serve:** Serve over cooked egg noodles.

Vegetarian Chili

Ingredients:

- 1 tbsp oil
- 1 onion, chopped
- 2 cloves garlic, minced
- 1 bell pepper, chopped
- 2 cans (15 oz) kidney beans, drained
- 1 can (15 oz) black beans, drained
- 1 can (15 oz) diced tomatoes
- 2 tbsp chili powder
- 1 tsp cumin
- Salt and pepper to taste

Instructions:

1. **Sauté Veggies:** Heat oil in a large pot over medium heat. Add onion, garlic, and bell pepper; sauté until softened.
2. **Add Ingredients:** Stir in beans, diced tomatoes, chili powder, cumin, salt, and pepper.
3. **Simmer:** Bring to a boil, then reduce heat and simmer for 20-30 minutes.
4. **Serve:** Enjoy hot, garnished with cheese or sour cream if desired.

Shrimp Scampi

Ingredients:

- 1 lb shrimp, peeled and deveined
- 8 oz linguine or spaghetti
- 4 cloves garlic, minced
- 1/2 cup white wine or chicken broth
- 1/4 cup butter
- 1/4 cup olive oil
- 1/4 tsp red pepper flakes (optional)
- Juice of 1 lemon
- Fresh parsley, chopped (for garnish)

Instructions:

1. **Cook Pasta:** Boil salted water and cook pasta according to package instructions; drain and set aside.
2. **Sauté Shrimp:** In a large skillet, melt butter and olive oil over medium heat. Add garlic and red pepper flakes, cooking until fragrant.
3. **Add Shrimp:** Add shrimp and cook until pink, about 3-4 minutes.
4. **Make Sauce:** Stir in white wine, lemon juice, and cooked pasta; toss to combine.
5. **Serve:** Garnish with fresh parsley and serve immediately.

Ratatouille

Ingredients:

- 1 eggplant, diced
- 1 zucchini, diced
- 1 bell pepper, diced
- 1 onion, chopped
- 3 cloves garlic, minced
- 1 can (15 oz) diced tomatoes
- 2 tbsp olive oil
- 1 tsp dried thyme
- Salt and pepper to taste

Instructions:

1. **Sauté Veggies:** Heat olive oil in a large pot. Add onion and garlic; sauté until softened.
2. **Add Vegetables:** Add eggplant, zucchini, and bell pepper. Cook until tender.
3. **Add Tomatoes:** Stir in diced tomatoes, thyme, salt, and pepper.
4. **Simmer:** Simmer for 20-30 minutes until the flavors meld.
5. **Serve:** Enjoy hot as a side or over rice.

Pork Tenderloin with Apples

Ingredients:

- 1 lb pork tenderloin
- 2 apples, sliced
- 1 onion, sliced
- 2 tbsp olive oil
- 1 tsp thyme
- Salt and pepper to taste

Instructions:

1. **Preheat Oven:** Preheat the oven to 400°F (200°C).
2. **Sear Pork:** In an oven-safe skillet, heat olive oil over medium-high heat. Season pork with salt and pepper; sear on all sides until browned.
3. **Add Apples and Onions:** Add apple slices and onion to the skillet. Sprinkle with thyme.
4. **Bake:** Transfer to the oven and bake for 20-25 minutes, until the pork is cooked through.
5. **Serve:** Slice pork and serve with the apple and onion mixture.

Creamy Mushroom Risotto

Ingredients:

- 1 cup Arborio rice
- 4 cups chicken or vegetable broth
- 1 onion, chopped
- 2 cloves garlic, minced
- 2 cups mushrooms, sliced
- 1/2 cup white wine (optional)
- 1/2 cup Parmesan cheese
- 2 tbsp butter
- Salt and pepper to taste

Instructions:

1. **Heat Broth:** In a saucepan, warm the broth over low heat.
2. **Sauté Veggies:** In a large pot, melt butter and sauté onion and garlic until softened. Add mushrooms and cook until browned.
3. **Add Rice:** Stir in Arborio rice and cook for 1-2 minutes.
4. **Add Wine:** Pour in white wine (if using) and stir until absorbed.
5. **Add Broth:** Gradually add warm broth, one ladle at a time, stirring frequently until absorbed before adding more. Repeat until rice is creamy and al dente.
6. **Finish:** Stir in Parmesan, salt, and pepper. Serve hot.

Enjoy preparing and savoring these delicious dishes!

Lemon Herb Grilled Chicken

Ingredients:

- 4 chicken breasts
- 1/4 cup olive oil
- Juice of 2 lemons
- 3 cloves garlic, minced
- 1 tsp dried oregano
- 1 tsp thyme
- Salt and pepper to taste

Instructions:

1. **Marinate Chicken:** In a bowl, whisk together olive oil, lemon juice, garlic, oregano, thyme, salt, and pepper. Add chicken breasts and marinate for at least 30 minutes.
2. **Preheat Grill:** Preheat the grill to medium-high heat.
3. **Grill Chicken:** Remove chicken from marinade and grill for 6-7 minutes on each side, or until cooked through.
4. **Serve:** Let rest for a few minutes, then slice and serve with your choice of sides.

Tofu Stir-Fry

Ingredients:

- 1 block firm tofu, pressed and cubed
- 2 cups mixed vegetables (bell peppers, broccoli, snap peas)
- 3 tbsp soy sauce
- 1 tbsp sesame oil
- 2 cloves garlic, minced
- 1 tsp ginger, minced
- Cooked rice or noodles for serving

Instructions:

1. **Sauté Tofu:** In a large skillet, heat sesame oil over medium heat. Add cubed tofu and cook until golden on all sides. Remove and set aside.
2. **Sauté Veggies:** In the same skillet, add garlic and ginger; sauté for 30 seconds. Add mixed vegetables and stir-fry until tender.
3. **Combine:** Return tofu to the skillet, add soy sauce, and toss to combine.
4. **Serve:** Serve over rice or noodles.

Fish Tacos with Cabbage Slaw

Ingredients:

- 1 lb white fish (cod, tilapia)
- 1 tbsp olive oil
- 1 tsp cumin
- 1 tsp paprika
- Salt and pepper to taste
- Corn tortillas
- 2 cups cabbage, shredded
- 1/4 cup cilantro, chopped
- Juice of 1 lime
- Optional: avocado and salsa for topping

Instructions:

1. **Season Fish:** Preheat oven to 400°F (200°C). Rub fish with olive oil, cumin, paprika, salt, and pepper. Bake for 12-15 minutes until cooked through.
2. **Make Slaw:** In a bowl, combine cabbage, cilantro, lime juice, salt, and pepper.
3. **Assemble Tacos:** Warm corn tortillas and fill with fish and cabbage slaw. Top with avocado and salsa if desired.

Quinoa Salad with Roasted Vegetables

Ingredients:

- 1 cup quinoa, rinsed
- 2 cups vegetable broth or water
- 2 cups assorted vegetables (zucchini, bell peppers, carrots), diced
- 2 tbsp olive oil
- 1 tsp garlic powder
- Salt and pepper to taste
- 1/4 cup feta cheese (optional)
- Fresh parsley for garnish

Instructions:

1. **Cook Quinoa:** In a pot, bring quinoa and broth to a boil. Reduce heat, cover, and simmer for 15 minutes. Fluff with a fork.
2. **Roast Vegetables:** Preheat oven to 425°F (220°C). Toss vegetables with olive oil, garlic powder, salt, and pepper. Roast for 20-25 minutes until tender.
3. **Combine:** In a large bowl, mix cooked quinoa and roasted vegetables. Top with feta cheese and garnish with parsley.

Baked Ziti

Ingredients:

- 1 lb ziti pasta
- 2 cups marinara sauce
- 2 cups ricotta cheese
- 2 cups shredded mozzarella cheese
- 1/2 cup grated Parmesan cheese
- 1 tsp Italian seasoning
- Salt and pepper to taste

Instructions:

1. **Preheat Oven:** Preheat the oven to 375°F (190°C).
2. **Cook Pasta:** Boil ziti according to package instructions until al dente; drain.
3. **Mix Ingredients:** In a bowl, combine cooked ziti, marinara sauce, ricotta, half of the mozzarella, Italian seasoning, salt, and pepper.
4. **Bake:** Transfer to a baking dish, top with remaining mozzarella and Parmesan. Bake for 25-30 minutes until bubbly and golden.

Stuffed Bell Peppers

Ingredients:

- 4 bell peppers (any color)
- 1 lb ground beef or turkey
- 1 cup cooked rice
- 1 can (15 oz) diced tomatoes
- 1 tsp Italian seasoning
- 1 cup shredded cheese (cheddar or mozzarella)

Instructions:

1. **Preheat Oven:** Preheat the oven to 375°F (190°C).
2. **Cook Meat:** In a skillet, cook ground meat until browned; drain excess fat.
3. **Mix Filling:** In a bowl, combine cooked meat, rice, diced tomatoes, Italian seasoning, and half of the cheese.
4. **Stuff Peppers:** Cut tops off bell peppers and remove seeds. Fill each pepper with the meat mixture.
5. **Bake:** Place in a baking dish, cover with foil, and bake for 30 minutes. Uncover, sprinkle with remaining cheese, and bake for an additional 10-15 minutes.

Thai Green Curry

Ingredients:

- 1 lb chicken or tofu, cubed
- 1 can (13.5 oz) coconut milk
- 2 tbsp green curry paste
- 2 cups mixed vegetables (bell peppers, eggplant, peas)
- 2 tbsp fish sauce or soy sauce
- Fresh basil for garnish
- Cooked rice for serving

Instructions:

1. **Cook Protein:** In a large pot, cook chicken or tofu until browned; remove and set aside.
2. **Make Sauce:** In the same pot, add coconut milk and green curry paste. Stir to combine and bring to a simmer.
3. **Add Veggies:** Add mixed vegetables and cook until tender. Return the chicken or tofu to the pot and stir in fish sauce or soy sauce.
4. **Serve:** Garnish with fresh basil and serve over rice.

Eggplant Parmesan

Ingredients:

- 1 large eggplant, sliced
- Salt (for sweating eggplant)
- 2 cups marinara sauce
- 2 cups shredded mozzarella cheese
- 1/2 cup grated Parmesan cheese
- 1 cup breadcrumbs
- Olive oil for frying

Instructions:

1. **Prepare Eggplant:** Sprinkle eggplant slices with salt and let sit for 30 minutes. Rinse and pat dry.
2. **Bread Eggplant:** Dredge slices in breadcrumbs. In a skillet, heat olive oil over medium heat. Fry eggplant until golden on both sides; drain on paper towels.
3. **Assemble:** In a baking dish, layer marinara sauce, fried eggplant, mozzarella, and Parmesan. Repeat layers, finishing with cheese on top.
4. **Bake:** Preheat oven to 375°F (190°C) and bake for 25-30 minutes until bubbly and golden.

Enjoy these delicious and satisfying meals!

Moroccan Chickpea Stew

Ingredients:

- 1 can (15 oz) chickpeas, drained and rinsed
- 1 onion, chopped
- 2 cloves garlic, minced
- 1 carrot, diced
- 1 bell pepper, diced
- 1 can (14 oz) diced tomatoes
- 2 cups vegetable broth
- 1 tsp cumin
- 1 tsp paprika
- 1/2 tsp cinnamon
- Salt and pepper to taste
- Fresh cilantro for garnish

Instructions:

1. **Sauté Veggies:** In a large pot, heat olive oil over medium heat. Add onion and garlic; sauté until softened.
2. **Add Vegetables:** Stir in carrot and bell pepper; cook for a few minutes.
3. **Add Spices:** Add cumin, paprika, cinnamon, salt, and pepper; stir to combine.
4. **Simmer:** Add chickpeas, diced tomatoes, and vegetable broth. Bring to a boil, then reduce heat and simmer for 20-25 minutes.
5. **Serve:** Garnish with fresh cilantro and serve hot.

Honey Garlic Salmon

Ingredients:

- 4 salmon fillets
- 1/4 cup honey
- 3 cloves garlic, minced
- 2 tbsp soy sauce
- 1 tbsp olive oil
- Salt and pepper to taste
- Lemon wedges for serving

Instructions:

1. **Preheat Oven:** Preheat the oven to 400°F (200°C).
2. **Make Marinade:** In a small bowl, whisk together honey, garlic, soy sauce, olive oil, salt, and pepper.
3. **Marinate Salmon:** Place salmon fillets in a baking dish and pour marinade over them. Let sit for 15 minutes.
4. **Bake:** Bake for 12-15 minutes until salmon is cooked through and flakes easily.
5. **Serve:** Serve with lemon wedges.

Chicken Fajitas

Ingredients:

- 1 lb chicken breast, sliced
- 1 onion, sliced
- 2 bell peppers, sliced
- 2 tbsp olive oil
- 2 tsp chili powder
- 1 tsp cumin
- Salt and pepper to taste
- Tortillas for serving
- Optional toppings: sour cream, avocado, salsa

Instructions:

1. **Sauté Chicken:** In a skillet, heat olive oil over medium-high heat. Add chicken and cook until browned; remove from skillet.
2. **Cook Veggies:** In the same skillet, add onion and bell peppers; sauté until tender.
3. **Combine:** Return chicken to the skillet, add chili powder, cumin, salt, and pepper; stir to combine and heat through.
4. **Serve:** Serve in tortillas with desired toppings.

Vegetable Pad Thai

Ingredients:

- 8 oz rice noodles
- 2 tbsp vegetable oil
- 2 cloves garlic, minced
- 1 cup mixed vegetables (carrots, bell peppers, broccoli)
- 2 eggs, lightly beaten
- 1/4 cup soy sauce
- 2 tbsp peanut butter
- 1 tbsp lime juice
- Chopped peanuts and cilantro for garnish

Instructions:

1. **Cook Noodles:** Cook rice noodles according to package instructions; drain and set aside.
2. **Sauté Veggies:** In a large skillet, heat oil over medium heat. Add garlic and mixed vegetables; stir-fry until tender.
3. **Add Eggs:** Push veggies to the side and pour in beaten eggs; scramble until cooked.
4. **Combine:** Add noodles, soy sauce, peanut butter, and lime juice; toss to combine and heat through.
5. **Serve:** Garnish with chopped peanuts and cilantro.

Beef and Broccoli Stir-Fry

Ingredients:

- 1 lb beef (flank or sirloin), sliced thin
- 2 cups broccoli florets
- 3 tbsp soy sauce
- 2 tbsp oyster sauce (optional)
- 2 cloves garlic, minced
- 1 tbsp ginger, minced
- 2 tbsp vegetable oil
- Cooked rice for serving

Instructions:

1. **Cook Beef:** In a skillet or wok, heat oil over medium-high heat. Add beef and stir-fry until browned; remove and set aside.
2. **Sauté Veggies:** In the same skillet, add garlic and ginger; stir-fry for 30 seconds. Add broccoli and a splash of water; cover and steam for 2-3 minutes.
3. **Combine:** Return beef to the skillet, add soy sauce and oyster sauce; stir to combine and heat through.
4. **Serve:** Serve over cooked rice.

Butternut Squash Soup

Ingredients:

- 1 butternut squash, peeled and cubed
- 1 onion, chopped
- 2 cloves garlic, minced
- 4 cups vegetable broth
- 1 tsp thyme
- Salt and pepper to taste
- Olive oil for sautéing

Instructions:

1. **Sauté Onion:** In a large pot, heat olive oil over medium heat. Add onion and garlic; sauté until softened.
2. **Add Squash:** Add cubed butternut squash, thyme, salt, and pepper; stir to combine.
3. **Add Broth:** Pour in vegetable broth and bring to a boil. Reduce heat and simmer for 20-25 minutes until squash is tender.
4. **Blend:** Use an immersion blender or regular blender to puree the soup until smooth.
5. **Serve:** Serve hot, garnished with a drizzle of olive oil if desired.

Shrimp and Grits

Ingredients:

- 1 cup grits
- 4 cups water or chicken broth
- 1 lb shrimp, peeled and deveined
- 4 slices bacon, chopped
- 2 cloves garlic, minced
- 1/2 cup heavy cream
- 1/4 cup green onions, sliced
- Salt and pepper to taste

Instructions:

1. **Cook Grits:** In a pot, bring water or broth to a boil. Stir in grits and cook according to package instructions until creamy.
2. **Cook Bacon:** In a skillet, cook bacon until crispy; remove and set aside, leaving the drippings.
3. **Sauté Shrimp:** In the same skillet, add garlic and shrimp; cook until shrimp are pink. Stir in heavy cream, salt, and pepper.
4. **Serve:** Serve shrimp over grits, garnished with bacon and green onions.

Caprese Salad

Ingredients:

- 4 large tomatoes, sliced
- 1 lb fresh mozzarella, sliced
- Fresh basil leaves
- 2 tbsp olive oil
- Balsamic vinegar (optional)
- Salt and pepper to taste

Instructions:

1. **Layer Ingredients:** On a serving platter, alternate slices of tomato and mozzarella.
2. **Add Basil:** Tuck basil leaves between the layers.
3. **Drizzle:** Drizzle with olive oil and balsamic vinegar, if using. Season with salt and pepper.
4. **Serve:** Serve fresh as a side or appetizer.

Teriyaki Chicken Bowls

Ingredients:

- 1 lb chicken breast, diced
- 1 cup broccoli florets
- 1 cup bell peppers, sliced
- 1/2 cup teriyaki sauce
- Cooked rice for serving
- Sesame seeds and green onions for garnish

Instructions:

1. **Cook Chicken:** In a skillet, cook diced chicken until browned and cooked through.
2. **Add Veggies:** Add broccoli and bell peppers; stir-fry until tender.
3. **Add Sauce:** Pour in teriyaki sauce and toss to coat. Cook for another 2-3 minutes.
4. **Serve:** Serve over cooked rice, garnished with sesame seeds and green onions.

Enjoy these flavorful dishes!

Black Bean Tacos

Ingredients:

- 1 can (15 oz) black beans, drained and rinsed
- 1 tsp cumin
- 1 tsp chili powder
- Salt and pepper to taste
- Corn or flour tortillas
- Toppings: diced tomatoes, avocado, cilantro, lime wedges

Instructions:

1. **Heat Beans:** In a saucepan, heat black beans over medium heat. Add cumin, chili powder, salt, and pepper; mash slightly.
2. **Warm Tortillas:** Warm tortillas in a skillet or microwave.
3. **Assemble Tacos:** Fill tortillas with black bean mixture and your choice of toppings. Serve with lime wedges.

Spinach and Feta Stuffed Chicken

Ingredients:

- 4 chicken breasts
- 1 cup fresh spinach, chopped
- 1/2 cup feta cheese, crumbled
- 2 cloves garlic, minced
- 1 tsp oregano
- Salt and pepper to taste
- Olive oil for drizzling

Instructions:

1. **Preheat Oven:** Preheat oven to 375°F (190°C).
2. **Prepare Filling:** In a bowl, combine spinach, feta, garlic, oregano, salt, and pepper.
3. **Stuff Chicken:** Cut a pocket in each chicken breast and fill with the spinach mixture.
4. **Bake:** Place chicken in a baking dish, drizzle with olive oil, and bake for 25-30 minutes until cooked through.

Lasagna Bolognese

Ingredients:

- 12 lasagna noodles
- 1 lb ground beef or turkey
- 1 onion, chopped
- 2 cloves garlic, minced
- 1 can (28 oz) crushed tomatoes
- 2 cups ricotta cheese
- 2 cups shredded mozzarella cheese
- 1/2 cup grated Parmesan cheese
- 1 tsp Italian seasoning
- Salt and pepper to taste

Instructions:

1. **Cook Meat:** In a skillet, cook ground meat with onion and garlic until browned. Drain excess fat.
2. **Add Sauce:** Stir in crushed tomatoes, Italian seasoning, salt, and pepper. Simmer for 10 minutes.
3. **Boil Noodles:** Cook lasagna noodles according to package instructions; drain.
4. **Assemble:** In a baking dish, layer meat sauce, noodles, ricotta, and mozzarella. Repeat layers, finishing with mozzarella and Parmesan on top.
5. **Bake:** Preheat oven to 375°F (190°C) and bake for 30-35 minutes until bubbly and golden.

Greek Salad with Grilled Chicken

Ingredients:

- 2 chicken breasts
- 6 cups mixed greens
- 1 cucumber, diced
- 1 cup cherry tomatoes, halved
- 1/2 cup red onion, thinly sliced
- 1/2 cup Kalamata olives
- 1/2 cup feta cheese, crumbled
- Olive oil, lemon juice, salt, and pepper for dressing

Instructions:

1. **Grill Chicken:** Season chicken with olive oil, salt, and pepper. Grill until cooked through; let rest, then slice.
2. **Prepare Salad:** In a large bowl, combine mixed greens, cucumber, tomatoes, red onion, olives, and feta.
3. **Dress Salad:** Drizzle with olive oil and lemon juice; toss to combine.
4. **Serve:** Top salad with sliced grilled chicken.

Coconut Curry Lentil Soup

Ingredients:

- 1 cup lentils, rinsed
- 1 can (13.5 oz) coconut milk
- 4 cups vegetable broth
- 1 onion, chopped
- 2 cloves garlic, minced
- 1 tbsp curry powder
- 1 tsp ginger, minced
- Salt and pepper to taste
- Fresh cilantro for garnish

Instructions:

1. **Sauté Onions:** In a pot, heat olive oil over medium heat. Add onion, garlic, and ginger; sauté until softened.
2. **Add Ingredients:** Stir in curry powder, lentils, coconut milk, and vegetable broth. Bring to a boil.
3. **Simmer:** Reduce heat and simmer for 25-30 minutes until lentils are tender.
4. **Serve:** Season with salt and pepper; garnish with fresh cilantro.

BBQ Pulled Pork Sandwiches

Ingredients:

- 2 lbs pork shoulder
- 1 cup BBQ sauce
- 1 onion, sliced
- Salt and pepper to taste
- Sandwich buns for serving
- Coleslaw for topping (optional)

Instructions:

1. **Cook Pork:** In a slow cooker, place pork shoulder and sliced onion. Season with salt and pepper, and pour BBQ sauce over the top.
2. **Slow Cook:** Cook on low for 8 hours or until pork is tender and shreds easily.
3. **Shred Pork:** Remove pork, shred with two forks, and mix with remaining BBQ sauce.
4. **Serve:** Serve on sandwich buns, topped with coleslaw if desired.

Pesto Pasta Primavera

Ingredients:

- 8 oz pasta (your choice)
- 2 cups mixed vegetables (zucchini, bell peppers, carrots)
- 1/2 cup pesto sauce
- Olive oil for sautéing
- Grated Parmesan cheese for serving

Instructions:

1. **Cook Pasta:** Cook pasta according to package instructions; drain and set aside.
2. **Sauté Vegetables:** In a skillet, heat olive oil over medium heat. Add mixed vegetables and sauté until tender.
3. **Combine:** Toss cooked pasta with sautéed vegetables and pesto sauce until well coated.
4. **Serve:** Serve warm, topped with grated Parmesan cheese.

Balsamic Glazed Brussels Sprouts

Ingredients:

- 1 lb Brussels sprouts, halved
- 2 tbsp olive oil
- 1/4 cup balsamic vinegar
- Salt and pepper to taste
- 1/4 cup grated Parmesan cheese (optional)

Instructions:

1. **Preheat Oven:** Preheat the oven to 400°F (200°C).
2. **Prepare Brussels Sprouts:** Toss Brussels sprouts with olive oil, balsamic vinegar, salt, and pepper.
3. **Roast:** Spread on a baking sheet and roast for 20-25 minutes until tender and caramelized.
4. **Serve:** Drizzle with additional balsamic if desired and sprinkle with Parmesan cheese.

Chicken Caesar Salad

Ingredients:

- 2 chicken breasts
- 6 cups romaine lettuce, chopped
- 1/2 cup Caesar dressing
- 1/2 cup croutons
- 1/4 cup grated Parmesan cheese

Instructions:

1. **Grill Chicken:** Season chicken with olive oil, salt, and pepper. Grill until cooked through; let rest, then slice.
2. **Prepare Salad:** In a large bowl, combine romaine lettuce, Caesar dressing, and croutons. Toss to combine.
3. **Serve:** Top salad with sliced grilled chicken and sprinkle with Parmesan cheese.

Enjoy these delicious meals!

Vegetable Samosas

Ingredients:

- **For the Filling:**
    - 2 cups potatoes, peeled and cubed
    - 1 cup peas (fresh or frozen)
    - 1 onion, chopped
    - 2 cloves garlic, minced
    - 1 tsp cumin
    - 1 tsp coriander
    - 1/2 tsp garam masala
    - Salt and pepper to taste
    - Oil for frying
- **For the Dough:**
    - 2 cups all-purpose flour
    - 1/4 cup oil
    - 1/2 tsp salt
    - Water as needed

Instructions:

1. **Prepare Filling:** Boil potatoes until tender; mash and mix with peas, onion, garlic, spices, salt, and pepper.
2. **Make Dough:** Combine flour, oil, and salt in a bowl. Gradually add water to form a soft dough; let rest for 30 minutes.
3. **Shape Samosas:** Divide dough into small balls, roll out into circles, and cut in half. Form cones and fill with the vegetable mixture; seal edges.
4. **Fry:** Heat oil in a deep pan. Fry samosas until golden brown. Drain on paper towels.

Salmon Quinoa Bowl

Ingredients:

- 2 salmon fillets
- 1 cup quinoa, rinsed
- 2 cups vegetable broth
- 1 cup cherry tomatoes, halved
- 1 avocado, sliced
- 1/4 cup fresh parsley, chopped
- Olive oil, lemon juice, salt, and pepper to taste

Instructions:

1. **Cook Quinoa:** In a pot, bring quinoa and vegetable broth to a boil. Reduce heat, cover, and simmer for 15 minutes. Fluff with a fork.
2. **Cook Salmon:** Season salmon with olive oil, salt, and pepper. Grill or bake at 400°F (200°C) for 12-15 minutes until cooked through.
3. **Assemble Bowls:** In bowls, layer quinoa, salmon, cherry tomatoes, and avocado. Drizzle with olive oil and lemon juice. Garnish with parsley.

Chorizo and Potato Hash

Ingredients:

- 1 lb chorizo sausage, casings removed
- 2 cups potatoes, diced
- 1 onion, chopped
- 1 bell pepper, diced
- 2 cloves garlic, minced
- Salt and pepper to taste
- Fresh cilantro for garnish

Instructions:

1. **Cook Potatoes:** Boil diced potatoes until just tender; drain.
2. **Cook Chorizo:** In a skillet, cook chorizo over medium heat until browned; remove and set aside.
3. **Sauté Veggies:** In the same skillet, add onion, bell pepper, and garlic; sauté until softened.
4. **Combine:** Add potatoes and cooked chorizo; cook until crispy and heated through. Season with salt and pepper. Garnish with cilantro.

Indian Butter Chicken

Ingredients:

- 1 lb chicken breast, cubed
- 1 onion, chopped
- 3 cloves garlic, minced
- 1 tbsp ginger, minced
- 1 can (14 oz) crushed tomatoes
- 1 cup heavy cream
- 1/4 cup butter
- 2 tbsp garam masala
- 1 tsp cumin
- Salt to taste
- Cooked rice for serving

Instructions:

1. **Cook Chicken:** In a skillet, melt butter over medium heat. Add onion, garlic, and ginger; sauté until softened.
2. **Add Chicken:** Add chicken and cook until browned.
3. **Make Sauce:** Stir in crushed tomatoes, heavy cream, garam masala, cumin, and salt. Simmer for 20 minutes until chicken is cooked through.
4. **Serve:** Serve with cooked rice.

Zucchini Noodles with Marinara

Ingredients:

- 4 medium zucchini, spiralized
- 2 cups marinara sauce
- 2 cloves garlic, minced
- Olive oil for sautéing
- Fresh basil for garnish
- Grated Parmesan cheese for serving

Instructions:

1. **Sauté Zoodles:** In a skillet, heat olive oil over medium heat. Add garlic and zucchini noodles; sauté for 2-3 minutes until just tender.
2. **Add Sauce:** Stir in marinara sauce and heat through.
3. **Serve:** Serve topped with fresh basil and grated Parmesan cheese.

Falafel Wraps

Ingredients:

- **For the Falafel:**
    - 1 can (15 oz) chickpeas, drained
    - 1 onion, chopped
    - 2 cloves garlic, minced
    - 1/4 cup parsley, chopped
    - 1 tsp cumin
    - 1/2 tsp coriander
    - Salt and pepper to taste
    - Oil for frying
- **For the Wraps:**
    - Pita bread or tortillas
    - Lettuce, tomato, cucumber, and tahini sauce for serving

Instructions:

1. **Make Falafel Mixture:** In a food processor, blend chickpeas, onion, garlic, parsley, and spices until combined but still chunky.
2. **Shape and Fry:** Form mixture into balls or patties. Fry in hot oil until golden brown. Drain on paper towels.
3. **Assemble Wraps:** Fill pita or tortillas with falafel, lettuce, tomato, cucumber, and tahini sauce.

Sweet Potato and Black Bean Enchiladas

Ingredients:

- 2 cups sweet potatoes, peeled and diced
- 1 can (15 oz) black beans, drained
- 1 tsp cumin
- 1 tsp chili powder
- 8 corn tortillas
- 2 cups enchilada sauce
- 1 cup shredded cheese (cheddar or Monterey Jack)

Instructions:

1. **Cook Sweet Potatoes:** Boil sweet potatoes until tender; drain and mash. Mix with black beans, cumin, and chili powder.
2. **Fill Tortillas:** Preheat oven to 375°F (190°C). Fill each tortilla with the sweet potato mixture and roll up; place seam-side down in a baking dish.
3. **Add Sauce and Cheese:** Pour enchilada sauce over the top and sprinkle with cheese.
4. **Bake:** Bake for 20-25 minutes until cheese is bubbly.

Cilantro Lime Rice with Grilled Shrimp

Ingredients:

- 1 cup rice
- 2 cups water or chicken broth
- 1 lb shrimp, peeled and deveined
- 1/4 cup cilantro, chopped
- Juice of 1 lime
- Olive oil, salt, and pepper to taste

Instructions:

1. **Cook Rice:** In a pot, bring rice and water or broth to a boil. Reduce heat, cover, and simmer for 15 minutes. Fluff with a fork and stir in cilantro and lime juice.
2. **Grill Shrimp:** Toss shrimp with olive oil, salt, and pepper. Grill on medium-high heat for 2-3 minutes per side until cooked through.
3. **Serve:** Serve grilled shrimp over cilantro lime rice.

Enjoy these flavorful and satisfying dishes!

Beef Enchiladas

Ingredients:

- 1 lb ground beef
- 1 onion, chopped
- 2 cloves garlic, minced
- 1 can (15 oz) black beans, drained
- 1 cup enchilada sauce
- 8 corn tortillas
- 2 cups shredded cheese (cheddar or Mexican blend)
- 1 tsp cumin
- 1 tsp chili powder
- Fresh cilantro for garnish

Instructions:

1. **Preheat Oven:** Preheat oven to 375°F (190°C).
2. **Cook Beef:** In a skillet, cook ground beef, onion, and garlic until browned. Drain excess fat. Stir in black beans, cumin, chili powder, and 1/2 cup enchilada sauce.
3. **Fill Tortillas:** Fill each tortilla with the beef mixture, roll up, and place seam-side down in a baking dish.
4. **Add Sauce and Cheese:** Pour remaining enchilada sauce over the top and sprinkle with cheese.
5. **Bake:** Bake for 20-25 minutes until cheese is bubbly. Garnish with cilantro.

Roasted Vegetable Quiche

Ingredients:

- 1 pre-made pie crust
- 1 cup mixed vegetables (bell peppers, zucchini, onions), roasted
- 4 eggs
- 1 cup milk
- 1 cup shredded cheese (cheddar or Swiss)
- Salt and pepper to taste
- Fresh herbs (thyme or parsley) for garnish

Instructions:

1. **Preheat Oven:** Preheat oven to 375°F (190°C).
2. **Prepare Crust:** Place pie crust in a pie dish.
3. **Mix Filling:** In a bowl, whisk together eggs, milk, salt, and pepper. Stir in roasted vegetables and cheese.
4. **Bake:** Pour filling into the crust and bake for 30-35 minutes until set.
5. **Serve:** Garnish with fresh herbs and serve warm.

Mediterranean Grain Bowl

Ingredients:

- 1 cup quinoa or farro, cooked
- 1 cup cherry tomatoes, halved
- 1 cucumber, diced
- 1/2 cup Kalamata olives, pitted and halved
- 1/4 cup feta cheese, crumbled
- 2 tbsp olive oil
- 1 tbsp red wine vinegar
- Fresh parsley for garnish
- Salt and pepper to taste

Instructions:

1. **Combine Ingredients:** In a large bowl, combine cooked grains, tomatoes, cucumber, olives, and feta cheese.
2. **Dress Salad:** In a small bowl, whisk together olive oil, red wine vinegar, salt, and pepper. Pour over the grain mixture and toss to combine.
3. **Serve:** Garnish with fresh parsley and serve chilled or at room temperature.

Jambalaya

Ingredients:

- 1 lb chicken breast, diced
- 1 lb shrimp, peeled and deveined
- 1 onion, chopped
- 1 bell pepper, chopped
- 2 cloves garlic, minced
- 1 can (14 oz) diced tomatoes
- 1 cup long-grain rice
- 3 cups chicken broth
- 2 tsp Cajun seasoning
- Salt and pepper to taste

Instructions:

1. **Sauté Ingredients:** In a large pot, heat olive oil over medium heat. Add onion, bell pepper, and garlic; sauté until softened.
2. **Cook Chicken:** Add diced chicken and cook until browned.
3. **Add Rice and Broth:** Stir in rice, diced tomatoes, chicken broth, Cajun seasoning, salt, and pepper. Bring to a boil, then reduce heat and simmer for 20-25 minutes until rice is cooked.
4. **Add Shrimp:** Stir in shrimp during the last 5 minutes of cooking.
5. **Serve:** Serve hot, garnished with green onions if desired.

Lobster Mac and Cheese

Ingredients:

- 8 oz elbow macaroni
- 2 cups shredded cheese (cheddar and Gruyère)
- 2 cups milk
- 1/4 cup butter
- 1/4 cup flour
- 1 cup cooked lobster meat, chopped
- 1/2 tsp paprika
- Salt and pepper to taste

Instructions:

1. **Cook Pasta:** Cook macaroni according to package instructions; drain and set aside.
2. **Make Cheese Sauce:** In a saucepan, melt butter over medium heat. Whisk in flour and cook for 1-2 minutes. Gradually whisk in milk, stirring until thickened.
3. **Add Cheese:** Stir in shredded cheese until melted and smooth. Season with paprika, salt, and pepper.
4. **Combine:** Fold in cooked macaroni and lobster meat.
5. **Bake (optional):** Transfer to a baking dish, top with extra cheese, and bake at 350°F (175°C) for 20 minutes until bubbly.

Stuffed Portobello Mushrooms

Ingredients:

- 4 large portobello mushrooms
- 1 cup cooked quinoa
- 1/2 cup spinach, chopped
- 1/2 cup feta cheese, crumbled
- 1/4 cup sun-dried tomatoes, chopped
- 2 cloves garlic, minced
- Olive oil for drizzling
- Salt and pepper to taste

Instructions:

1. **Preheat Oven:** Preheat oven to 375°F (190°C).
2. **Prepare Filling:** In a bowl, combine cooked quinoa, spinach, feta, sun-dried tomatoes, garlic, salt, and pepper.
3. **Stuff Mushrooms:** Place portobello mushrooms on a baking sheet and fill each with the quinoa mixture. Drizzle with olive oil.
4. **Bake:** Bake for 20-25 minutes until mushrooms are tender.
5. **Serve:** Serve warm as an appetizer or main dish.

Chicken Noodle Soup

Ingredients:

- 1 lb chicken breast
- 4 cups chicken broth
- 2 cups egg noodles
- 2 carrots, sliced
- 2 celery stalks, sliced
- 1 onion, chopped
- 2 cloves garlic, minced
- Salt and pepper to taste
- Fresh parsley for garnish

Instructions:

1. **Cook Chicken:** In a large pot, combine chicken breast and broth. Bring to a boil, then simmer until chicken is cooked through; remove and shred.
2. **Sauté Veggies:** In the same pot, add onion, carrots, celery, and garlic; sauté until softened.
3. **Add Noodles:** Stir in egg noodles and cook until tender.
4. **Combine:** Return shredded chicken to the pot, season with salt and pepper, and simmer for a few more minutes.
5. **Serve:** Garnish with fresh parsley before serving.

Spicy Peanut Noodles

Ingredients:

- 8 oz noodles (spaghetti or rice noodles)
- 1/4 cup peanut butter
- 2 tbsp soy sauce
- 1 tbsp honey or maple syrup
- 1 tbsp sriracha (adjust to taste)
- 2 cloves garlic, minced
- 1 cup mixed vegetables (carrots, bell peppers, broccoli)
- Chopped peanuts and cilantro for garnish

Instructions:

1. **Cook Noodles:** Cook noodles according to package instructions; drain and set aside.
2. **Make Sauce:** In a bowl, whisk together peanut butter, soy sauce, honey, sriracha, and garlic until smooth.
3. **Sauté Veggies:** In a skillet, sauté mixed vegetables until tender.
4. **Combine:** Add cooked noodles and sauce to the skillet, tossing to combine.
5. **Serve:** Serve warm, garnished with chopped peanuts and cilantro.

Enjoy these delicious and hearty dishes!

www.ingramcontent.com/pod-product-compliance
Lightning Source LLC
LaVergne TN
LVHW081335060526
838201LV00055B/2662